ENDORSEMENTS

I'm a pastor. When my phone rings, I ⎡
possibility that the call could be heartl
every heartbreaking call involves a family in some way.
I don't know what your ACE score is, but this study will
bring you hope and healing that comes straight from
the pages of the Bible. Rene and Tim do not sugar-coat
how sin has led to massive dysfunction in the families
in Genesis. And if we are honest, we see that dysfunction in our own families. This study is engaging, and
the questions probe both the heart and the mind. May
you find restoration as you explore God's purpose for
families from the very beginning.

—Jason Arens, Lead Pastor
The Journey | South County, St. Louis, Missouri

Rene and Pastor Tim have done the church a great
service by connecting some of the most well-known
stories of our faith with the very real issues facing
children and families today. In their study, *Family:
It's Complicated!—a Bible Study of Adverse Childhood
Experiences in Genesis*, they have blended excellent
biblical scholarship with the science of adversity and
trauma in childhood. The result is a very accessible and
applicable guide through Genesis' dysfunctional families and relational dynamics that will impress small
groups and Sunday school classes with how relevant
these issues are today! I am grateful for the healing
and hope that God will bring to those individuals and

groups who choose to engage this study, and I could not recommend it more highly.

—Rev. Dr. Chris Haughee
Chaplain of Intermountain Residential Services in
Helena, Montana
Author of *Bruised Reeds and Smoldering Wicks*

Before there were nations, political parties, and government, there was family—God's glue for future generations. As goes the family, so goes the society. A short glimpse of our time indicates the foundations are crumbling. Why? No glue. To help stop the collapse, Rene Howitt and Tim Wesemann have authored an intensely practical and useful resource to help families in crisis work through the origins and symptoms of a family falling apart, and to give hope and next steps in restoring the foundations of a healthy and functioning family. Pastors and churches will find this resource a practical and profitable tool to use often in building healthy families. I commend this timely resource to help in gluing our families back together.

—Marion Hunerdosse, Lead Pastor
Flack Church, Excelsior Springs, Missouri
Heartland Conference of Churches

FAMILY

It's Complicated

A Bible study of adverse childhood experiences in Genesis

FAMILY

It's Complicated

A Bible study of adverse childhood experiences in Genesis

Rene Howitt & Tim Wesemann

REDEMPTION
PRESS

Published by Redemption Press, PO Box 427, Enumclaw, WA 98022

Toll Free (844) 2REDEEM (273-3336)

Redemption Press is honored to present this title in partnership with the author. The views expressed or implied in this work are those of the author. Redemption Press provides our imprint seal representing design excellence, creative content, and high quality production.

Unless otherwise noted, all Scripture is taken from the English Standard Version of the Bible.

English Standard Version (ESV)
The Holy Bible, English Standard Version. ESV® Text Edition: 2016. Copyright © 2001 by Crossway Bibles, a publishing ministry of Good News Publishers.

The Message (MSG)
Copyright © 1993, 1994, 1995, 1996, 2000, 2001, 2002 by Eugene H. Peterson

New International Version (NIV)
Holy Bible, New International Version®, NIV® Copyright ©1973, 1978, 1984, 2011 by Biblica Inc.® used by permission. All rights reserved worldwide.

ISBN 13: 978-1-68314-701-5
          978-1-68314-706-0 (ePub)
          978-1-68314-707-7 (Mobi)

Library of Congress Catalog Card Number: 2018958745

CONTENTS

PURPOSE

Recommended Reading before You Begin the Study

THANK YOU FOR PARTICIPATING in this Bible study centered on several families in the book of Genesis and relating their stories to families today—our families, our stories—and God's perfect grace that covers us all.

The Bible doesn't sugarcoat the realistic, sometimes shocking actions of God's people. But don't miss the astonishing, undeserved love God has for his people. That same amazing grace is ours through Jesus Christ, even in the most horrific situations of our lives and the world.

This study works side by side with a highly regarded study of Adverse Childhood Experiences, referred to as ACEs. The simple but insightful ACEs survey (included in this introduction) will prove helpful for this study, your own personal struggles, and the freeing help that comes from the undeserved love of Jesus Christ.

As you go through the Bible study, please understand that these biblical families lived in a different time and culture, and circumstances that are completely foreign to us may have been commonplace for them. Of course, that doesn't mean God's laws don't apply to God's family in the past or the present. While we don't have day-to-day details for each story, we do want to apply the lessons learned to our lives, using a greater understanding of God's will and ways without reading too much into certain situations.

From the first book of the Bible to reading today's headlines, we see the results of a sin-filled, broken world. Addictions, abuse (domestic, emotional, and verbal), pornography, theft, hatred, poverty, immorality, homelessness, apathy, unplanned pregnancies, sexual assault, bullying, murder, self-centeredness, and single-parent homes surround us.

First Timothy speaks of this trouble. "But understand this, that in the last days there will come times of difficulty. For people will be lovers of self, lovers of money, proud, arrogant, abusive, disobedient to their parents, ungrateful, unholy, heartless, unappeasable, slanderous, without self-control, brutal, not loving good, treacherous, reckless, swollen with conceit, lovers of pleasure rather than lovers of God, having the appearance of godliness, but denying its power" (2 Timothy 3:1–5).

This isn't what God intended for his creation. Life went from perfect to a perfectly deadly mess when sin barged through the door of our lives and our homes, creating cycles of family dysfunction.

But it's not hopeless. Our God has a perfect plan for imperfect families and individuals. There is life-changing good news in the giver of hope, forgiveness, and peace. His name is Jesus. He knows you and loves you so much he gave up his life in your place so that you can know real hope and lasting peace. As God's family, we learn by looking at God's Word and our lives through the cross of Jesus Christ.

A Word from Rene Howitt, Founder of COPE24

As a child advocate and Christian, I believe it is imperative that faith-based communities understand the importance and impact of our life experiences. While our experiences are both good and bad, I believe faith-based communities should encourage discussions about the effects of Adverse Childhood Experiences (ACEs) by using family dysfunction in the book of Genesis as a starting point. The questions and discussion points from Genesis will help us consider our family of origin and childhood experiences. It's not just about *other people*—it's about other people in our families, as well as the person we see in the mirror.

And hopefully, you'll be led as individuals, a family, and groups to find ways to help, encourage, and serve others, especially those struggling in their own family situations and personal experiences. Discussing and facing our past (and present) circumstances in an honest manner is difficult, but the rewards can be beneficial to us, as well as a blessing to future generations.

As you walk through this study, COPE24 wants you to promote a safe environment for sharing within your group. You need to provide a place where people can reveal openly and confidently the broken areas of their lives if they choose, without judgment or condemnation. Commit to confidentiality and respect. We encourage openness, vulnerability, and closeness in your discussion and prayer time. To this end, we ask that each participant agree to mutual confidentially by signing a covenant agreement below. (You may print as many copies as you need.)

CONFIDENTIALITY AGREEMENT

I will keep all private matters and conversations shared by my group members confidential at all times.

Name (printed):_____

Signed: _____

Date: _____

WHAT ARE ACEs
(ADVERSE CHILDHOOD
EXPERIENCES)?

IN THE 1990S, THERE was an extensive study conducted about Adverse Childhood Experiences. Drs. Vincent Felitte and Robert Anda began researching the correlation between child abuse and neglect and overall health.

From 1993 to 1996, an extremely diverse group of over 17,300 people participated in the ACEs study. Participants took the ACEs survey, consisting of ten questions with *Yes* or *No* answers. Each *Yes* counted as one point. The simple 0–10 score provides insights, focus, and help.

The most common issues confronted by child welfare were

- Abuse: physical, emotional, sexual
- Neglect: physical, emotional
- Family dysfunction: children living with parents suffering from serious mental health issues, parents suffering from addictions, the loss of a parent(s) due to divorce or incarceration, domestic violence

You are encouraged to take the ACEs survey on the next page before participating in this study.

ACEs Survey

Prior to your eighteenth birthday:
Did a parent or other adult in the household often or very often swear at you, insult you, put you down, humiliate you, or act in a way that made you afraid that you might be physically hurt?

No___   If Yes, enter 1 __

Did a parent or other adult in the household often or very often push, grab, slap, or throw something at you, or ever hit you so hard that you had marks or were injured?

No___   If Yes, enter 1 __

Did an adult or person at least five years older than you ever touch or fondle you or have you touch their body in a sexual way, or attempt or have oral, anal, or vaginal intercourse with you?

No___   If Yes, enter 1 __

Did you often or very often feel that no one in your family loved you or thought you were important or special, or that your family didn't look out for each other, feel close to each other, or support each other?

No___   If Yes, enter 1 __

Did you often or very often feel that you didn't have enough to eat, had to wear dirty clothes, had no one to protect you, or your parents were too drunk or high to take care of you or take you to the doctor if you needed it?

No____   If Yes, enter 1 __

Were your parents ever separated or divorced?

No____   If Yes, enter 1 __

Was your mother or stepmother often pushed, grabbed, slapped, or had something thrown at her, or sometimes, often, or very often kicked, bitten, hit with a fist, or hit with something hard, or ever repeatedly hit over at least a few minutes or threatened with a gun or knife?

No____   If Yes, enter 1 __

Did you live with anyone who was a problem drinker or alcoholic or who used street drugs?

No____   If Yes, enter 1 __

Was a household member depressed or mentally ill, or did a household member attempt suicide?

No____   If Yes, enter 1 __

Did a household member go to prison?

No____   If Yes, enter 1 __

Add up your "Yes" answers: _____ **This is your ACEs score**

ACES RESULTS FROM THE ORIGINAL STUDY:

- 64 percent had an ACEs score of at least one or more, concluding that 36 percent of us grew up in a home that could be described as "healthy"!
- 12.5 percent had an ACEs score of four or higher. No matter the combination of points, doctors find exponentially higher incidences of both physical and mental health conditions over a lifetime starting with a score of four.

Consider whether the adversities you faced as a child changed how you view the world, others, or yourself. Acknowledging and seeking to understand our adversities can lead to healing and change. Also, along with God's Word, the encouragement from trusted individuals, forgiveness, and peace can be found in God's presence and in his promises through Jesus Christ.

In the appendix, you'll find more information and resources regarding ACEs, coping mechanisms, dysfunction and family cycles, and medical concerns. You may also discover help and hope through a personal counselor and a discussion group.

May God richly bless your personal or group study.

Note: because the Bible readings for each session are lengthy, you are encouraged to read them before each meeting.

Lesson 1

THE GENESIS OF PROBLEMS: THE GENESIS OF HOPE

Read Genesis 3:1–24.

COULD ANYONE HAVE A greater reason to yell "Do over!" than Adam and Eve? They were gifted with a perfect world and a perfect relationship—with God, his creation, and each other. They had it all.

And then there was the tree and the tempting offer by the snake-oil salesman, Satan, in the shade of the tree. Then came the inward gaze instead of the upward gaze. The selfish decision. The fruit. The rejection of God's will. The bite. The spiraling, deadly fall into sin. The shattered image, and new, damaged, imperfect relationships—with God, his creation, and each other. So much for the perfect marriage. This was the genesis of all problems.

Immediately they experienced shame in their nakedness and in their actions. They played a round of hide-and-hope-he-doesn't-seek. The Lord won easily. Then the "game of life" brought a new challenge, fear.

Adam and Eve quickly invented another game, Blame: the First Edition.

In Genesis 3:11–13,

> The Lord God asked, "Who told you that you were naked? Have you eaten of the tree of which I commanded you not to eat?" The man said, "The woman whom you gave to be with me, she gave me fruit of the tree, and I ate." Then the Lord God said to the woman, "What is this that you have done?" The woman said, "The serpent deceived me, and I ate."

As God spoke, Adam and Eve stopped playing games. There were consequences for their actions. The serpent was cursed to the lowest esteem. The woman was promised great pain in childbirth. The man was promised pain through hard work to provide for his family and simply survive. And finally, death was promised for all humanity. "You are dust and to dust you shall return" (Genesis 3:19).

Their actions and the consequences that followed are the genesis of every sin and every problem. Every pain in our lives comes down to the presence of this sin that saturates the world. It's found in every news story that makes us cringe and in the skeletons of every family closet.

You see evidence of the results of sin in

- tears, fears, and pressure from peers;
- guilt grips and ego trips;
- headaches, heartaches, and earthquakes;
- AA and NA; EMS and PMS; STDs and MIAs;
- rape kits and clenched fists;
- jail cells and cancer cells; and
- foster homes, broken homes, and funeral homes.

Everyone and everything in this world are tainted by the results of sin, except for the Word of God, which offers good news for our sinful world and especially for our lives and our relationships. And amid seemingly hopeless words, God provides the gift of a sure and certain promise that is the genesis of hope in our lives and every life yet to be lived.

There is one who would come from the woman's seed (offspring) that would crush Satan's head and his power, but in the process, the heel of this promised savior-offspring would be bruised (paraphrased from Genesis 3:15).

And then the Lord drove Adam and Eve out of the Eden paradise he had created for them. But before he did, he made them garments of skins and clothed them. He exchanged their fig leaf loincloths for something more practical. What a gracious, compassionate act of love from a Father for his children who had turned their backs on him.

Consider that for a moment. A God who fashions clothes. A God who is a divine DIYer. A Father who loves and provides for his children. The creator of the heavens and earth kills one of the creatures he created and used its skin to cover his sinful children. Sound familiar? One day, in the future, this same heavenly Father would allow his Son to be killed so his children could be covered, wrapped in the righteousness, the perfection of the Son. The promised Savior. The promised offspring, born of a woman. Our Savior from sin and death. His name is Jesus.

Good verses of encouragement are found in Psalm 32:1–5:

> Blessed is the one whose transgression is forgiven, whose sin is covered. Blessed is the man against whom the Lord counts no iniquity, and in whose spirit there is no deceit. For when I kept silent, my bones wasted away through my groaning all day long. For day and night your hand was heavy upon me; my strength was dried up as by the heat of summer. I acknowledged my sin to you, and I did not cover my iniquity; I said, "I will confess my transgressions to the Lord," and you forgave the iniquity of my sin.

Consider. Discuss. Apply It to Your Life and Community.

If you could create the perfect marital or parental relationship, what would it look like?

_____

_____

_____

_____

How do the following feelings and reactions Adam and Eve experienced influence the families of today?

- blame
- shame
- regret
- anger
- failure
- resentment
- hope
- love and compassion

All these experiences and feelings were part of Adam and Eve's marital relationship and their individual lives before they became parents, and they brought those feelings, lessons, and memories with them into parenthood. Therefore, we need to remember and realize our past plays a significant role in our present lives. How might these past experiences and feelings become evident as Adam and Eve moved from this point forward?

How might their past have played a role as they raised their children?

_____

_____

_____

_____

What are some examples of how your past has played a role in your present life? Do you feel as though you've made decisions that have moved you out of your Garden of Eden? How have those decisions affected your relationships, including your relationship with God?

_____

_____

_____

_____

How does tension within marriages affect children? How had those tensions played a role in Adam and Eve's short- and long-term future within their relationships?

_____

_____

_____

_____

If you are a parent or may be one in the future, what harmful family cycles do you pray your children (and future generations) will break with God's help?

_____

_____

_____

_____

What Bible verses and promises encourage and bless you as you consider your relationships, harmful family cycles, and decisions? What role has forgiveness played in your growth and healing as a child of God? Take note of the verses and insights of others in your group, as they may provide help for you as the Holy Spirit grows your faith in Jesus.

_____

_____

_____

_____

Pray. Encourage. Move Forward, Filled with Hope.

In preparation for the next lesson, read Genesis 4:1–5:5.

Lesson 2

THE FIRST FAMILY: DEADLY DYNAMICS IN MAN'S IMAGE

Read Genesis 4:1–5:5.

EVE DISCOVERED THE MEANING of "multiplying pain in childbirth" when Cain their first-born arrived. It's a boy! It's a . . . well, just who is he? Understandably, Eve appears to think he is the fulfillment of the Lord's promise of one who would come from the woman's seed (offspring) and crush Satan's power (Genesis 3:15). At Cain's birth, Eve said, "I have gotten a man with the help of the Lord" (Genesis 4:1). Hebrew scholars (Hebrew is the original language of the Old Testament) note that the literal meaning of those words is, *I have gotten a man, namely, Yahweh (the Lord).*

Since we live on the other side of the cross, we know that promised Savior was Jesus, God's Son, and the offspring of a woman, Mary. Throughout the history of God's people, women have prayed for and wondered if her child would be the promised offspring. (Read what Noah's father said about his son in Genesis 5:28–29.)

This insight into Eve's words—that her child might be the promised child—adds so much to the story of the first family and their relationship dynamics. Let's not read too much into it, but after Eve's great proclamation about her revered firstborn, the next verse simply states, "And again, she bore his brother Abel" (Genesis 4:2).

With this supposition we can imagine what high expectations these parents had for their son. Did they talk to Cain about this *calling* they felt he had, albeit falsely? Cain's pride might have grown and resulted in arrogance. If so, consider the shockwaves this family experienced in Genesis 4:4–5 when the Lord had regard for Abel's offering but didn't pay attention to Cain's! Incidentally, Hebrews 11:4 tells us Abel's offering was given in faith, implying that Cain's was not. What an enormous disappointment for Cain and perhaps more for his parents, who held this false hope. And follow that up with this golden boy murdering his brother. Such a traumatic event would have crushed Adam and Eve, creating extreme grief over Abel's death as well as the death of their expectation that Cain was the promised one.

In Genesis 4:9–16, like his parents in the Garden of Eden, Cain added to his sin by making excuses to the Lord. And although there was a consequence for his deadly actions, the Lord continued to show he was a God of mercy and grace by protecting Cain. As Genesis 4 says,

> Cain said to the Lord, "Behold, you have driven me today away from the ground, and from your face I shall be hidden. I shall be a fugitive and a wanderer on the earth, and whoever finds me will kill me." Then the Lord said to him, "Not so! If anyone kills Cain, vengeance shall be taken on him sevenfold." (Genesis 4:9–16)

And like his parents who were exiled from the Garden of Eden because of their sin, Cain was exiled for his. Cain later married, had children, and headed a long line of descendants (Genesis 4:17–24). But the family cycle of great sin was portrayed in the lives of his descendants. We learn Lamech, a member of Cain's family tree, was a polygamist and a murderer (4:23–24). Sinful actions can pass from generation to generation. But with God's help, these actions can also be broken, freeing burdened individuals and families to live as new creations in Christ.

Adam and Eve were blessed with another son, Seth (4:25), along with other sons and daughters (5:4). And Scripture tells us, "When God created man, he made him in the likeness of God...When Adam had lived 130 years, *he fathered a son in his own likeness, after his image,* and named him Seth" (Genesis 5:1, 3, author's emphasis).

Our children are made in our own likenesses, our own broken, sinful images. And our children's children will be born similarly flawed. What a blessing to have a heavenly Father filled with mercy and grace who continues to care for us, his dearly loved children.

Consider. Discuss. Apply It to Your Life and Community.

Consider how parents may have false expectations for their children. Because each child is an individual with their own choices, a life can be unexpectedly turned upside down. What encouragement do you have for those dealing with disappointment? Examples include:

- The expectations of young parents that raising a child is easy. Sure, some dirty diapers and a crying fit occasionally, but nothing too serious. But then comes the colic, incessant crying, frayed nerves, extreme exhaustion, or desperation. And that's just the beginning.
- The godly family that surrounds their growing child with God's love and their own, expecting nothing but the best. But then comes an unexpected pregnancy, a DUI, the influence of ungodly friends, failing grades, suicidal tendencies, or rejection of Christ.

- Fill in your own examples.

  _____

  _____

  _____

  _____

What role does guilt play in families dealing with fighting, grief, or tragedy? How could that affect future generations?

  _____

  _____

  _____

  _____

How can sibling rivalry throw a family into turmoil? What might cause it? What encouragement do you have for those struggling with it in their lives?

  _____

  _____

  _____

  _____

How can we encourage and pray for youth who feel unloved or unimportant within their families to recognize their great worth in Christ's eyes and ours, passing that truth to future generations? Why might we consider replacing the term _self-esteem_ with _Christ-esteem_? Discuss this statement: when asking "Who is He (Jesus)?" you'll find the answer to "Who am I?" Be encouraged by reading Psalm 139:13–16; John 3:16; 1 John 1:8–9; Romans 8:31–39.

_____

_____

_____

_____

What is your reaction to God's caring response to Cain—mercy and grace—after Cain murdered his brother? What comfort do you find in his response based on your daily life? How is God's unconditional love and forgiveness speaking to you today in relation to how you respond to others, actions of hatred, anger, or even murder?

_____

_____

_____

_____

Consider the actions of the first family: Adam and Eve's sin and removal from paradise, tension between family members, questionable parenting choices, Abel's murder, and Cain's descendant murdering a man. Do you see this as coincidence or a possible cycle of dysfunction?

_____

_____

_____

_____

Pray. Encourage. Move Forward, Filled with Hope.

In preparation for the next lesson, read Genesis 4:17–24; 5:28–29; 6:5–10; 9:1–28.

Lesson 3

THE WATER AND THE WINE

Read Genesis 6:5–10; 9:1–27.

IN GENESIS 9:18–28, THE most common children's story about Noah familiar to us is filled with water, ark, and animals—the Great Flood in Genesis 6:13–8:22, which covered the earth, destroying all living things except for eight people from Noah's family who got aboard the ark before the flood.

Although we equate Noah with an ark and lots of water, he "found favor in the eyes of the Lord. Noah was a righteous man, blameless in his generation, and walked with God" (Genesis 6:8–9). Unlike Jesus, who was sinless, Noah wasn't sinless but walked closely with God as a man of faith. Noah was born with the sin that had passed down generation to generation from Adam and Eve. The prophet Jeremiah describes the heart as "deceitful above all things, and desperately sick; who can understand it?" (Jeremiah 17:9). Because his heart was deceitful, Noah needed to completely rely on God for righteousness because Jesus, the promised Messiah, had not come yet. God looked on Noah graciously and lovingly and found favor in him, just as the Father, through Jesus, looks graciously on us, his men, women, and children of faith.

Even though there are many biblical accounts about Noah, one story isn't included in children's Bible story books, painted as murals on nursery walls, or even in most conversations in church. The incident occured sometime after the waters from the flood had subsided, because Noah had not only cultivated his faith in God, but he had cultivated land and planted a vineyard. On this occasion Noah not only tasted his first fine wine, but he also got wasted on his vine's wine. He became inebriated, passed out, and was naked in his tent. Ham saw Noah in the tent, and instead of covering him up, Ham told his brothers. Scripture finishes the story: "Then Shem and Japheth took a garment, laid it on both their shoulders, and walked backward and covered the nakedness of their father. Their faces were turned backward, and they did not see their father's nakedness" (Genesis 9:23).

What a beautiful example of dealing with a loved one's sin found in Shem's and Japheth's actions (Galatians 6:1–2; 1 Peter 4:8). While Ham saw the sin of drunkenness, he brought dishonor and shame to his father by sharing it. You might say he attempted to bring his brothers into the sin. Ham did not act in love and did nothing helpful, and he brought shame to his father. Shem and Japheth honored their father by not witnessing the sin or their father's shame. Instead, they walked in backward to cover him. Their love covered their father and his sin.

Likewise, Jesus's sinless love, revealed through his horrific execution on the cross, covers the multitude of our sins today. More than that, he takes those sins on himself, as explained in 2 Corinthians 5:21: "For our sake he [God] made him [Jesus] to be sin who knew no sin, so that in him we might become the righteousness of God." Another great verse is also a comfort: "For the Lord is good; his steadfast love endures forever, and his faithfulness to all generations" (Psalm 100:5).

Genesis 4:17–24 and 5:28–29 provide an interesting side story about generational cycles and passing on family history. Noah's father, Lamech, knew that his ancestor, Cain, had murdered Abel. Several generations later, Lamech also murdered a man, knowing what the Lord had told Cain, as recorded in Genesis 4:15, 23–24. And it is likely that Lamech believed his son, Noah, was the offspring the Lord had promised Eve after the fall into sin (3:15; 5:29). Lamech said of Noah, "Out of the ground that the Lord has cursed, this one shall bring us relief from our work and from the painful toil of our hands." However, the Lord's promise of this savior-offspring would not be fulfilled until Jesus's birth.

Therefore, in Noah's day, "The Lord saw that the wickedness of man was great in the earth, and that every intention of the thoughts of his heart was only evil continually" (Genesis 6:5). Just as the people in Noah's day were completely entrenched in evil and sin, that same entrenchment of evil and sin could describe people today. And tomorrow. And until Christ returns. Yet God has given us his Word, which serves as a lamp to our feet and light to our path (Psalm 119:105). The Holy Spirit works through the life-giving Word of God that floods our lives with strength and wisdom for us to be able to walk with God.

Consider. Discuss. Apply It to Your Life and Community.

Prior to this study, when you took the ACEs Survey, question eight addressed alcohol and drugs. When excessive alcohol or drug use enters a situation, bad things usually happen. Add indignity, gossip, pornography, and the degradation of others to the substance abuse problem, and that results in a toxicity that affects (and often tears down) whole family units and even entire communities. Discuss how this might have affected you, your family, or your community.

_____

_____

_____

_____

Regarding man's sick heart *after* the flood, how do Genesis 8:21; Jeremiah 17:9; Psalm 14:1–3; Matthew 15:19; John 15:5; Romans 3:21–24; and Ephesians 2:8–9 support this teaching?

_____

_____

_____

_____

Do you think children learn more from their parents' words or their behavior?

_____

_____

_____

_____

Discuss the importance of parents teaching their children to respect others and how to properly respond to unhealthy or ungodly life choices. How might this be discussed or taught? What is the role of forgiveness and grace?

_____

_____

_____

_____

How has your view of your parents changed over the years? How have TV, social media, and the internet had an impact on your interaction in and compassion for the lives, problems, and sins of others?

_____

_____

_____

_____

What positive things have you learned from your parents (stepparents, grandparents, foster parents) about parenting?

_____

_____

_____

_____

Do you agree that Noah's sin or something similar applies to our world today? If so, we shouldn't be surprised at the sinful cycles of hate, abuse, neglect, jealousy, selfishness, and pride in families today. How can those generational cycles be broken? How can we, as parents, siblings, educators, and friends personally play a role in stopping the cycles? What hope does our Spirit-created faith have?

_____

_____

_____

_____

Discuss Galatians 6:1–2: "If anyone is caught in any transgression, you who are spiritual should restore him in a spirit of gentleness. Keep watch on yourself, lest you too be tempted. Bear one another's burdens, and so fulfill the law of Christ." How would you seek to build someone up and encourage them if they are struggling?

_____

_____

_____

_____

Pray. Encourage. Move Forward, Filled with Hope.

In preparation for the next lesson, read Genesis 11:27–32; 12:1–20 (and 20:1–6); 16:1–15; 17:1–21; 18:9–15; 21:1–14.

Lesson 4

ABRAM AND SARAI: THE LORD LISTENS, THE LORD SEES, AND WE LAUGH

Read Genesis 11:27–32; 12:1–20 (and 20:1–6); 16:1–15; 17:1–21; 18:9–15; 21:1–14.

THROUGHOUT THIS LESSON, WE will often refer to Abraham and Sarah by their original names because later in their lives, the Lord changed Abram's name to Abraham and the name of his wife, Sarai, to Sarah. Please realize they will be used interchangeably, and that is because of the name changes.

Since we have very little information about Abram and Sarai, these mini accounts below will explore the events as recorded in the Bible. Then we will discuss how they might apply to our lives today.

In Genesis 11:27–32, time had passed since the Lord first promised Abraham his family would grow into a great nation. This section provides you with some of the dynamics of Abram's family over the years.

- Terah had three sons: Abram (who married Sarai), Nahor, and Haran.
- Terah also served other gods, as noted in Joshua 24:2.
- Abram's brother, Haran, had a son, Lot, and daughters, Milcah and Iscah. He died in the presence of his father, Terah.
- Abram's brother, Nahor, married his niece, Milcah.
- Abram's mother had apparently died.
- Abram and Sarai, who was barren, provide familial care for their adult nephew, Lot.
- Grandfather (Terah), son and daughter-in-law (Abram and Sarai), and grandson (Lot) leave their home and travel (with servants and animals) to the new land of Canaan.

What are some possible challenges and blessings of multi-generational families living in one home?

_____

_____

_____

_____

Kinship providers in the US child welfare program are relatives or, in some cases, family friends who care for children who had to be removed from their birth parents. What family stress and conflict might the children, birth parents, and kinship providers experience?

_____

_____

_____

_____

In Genesis 12:1–20 and 20:1–6, at the Lord's leading, Abram traveled with his family by faith to Egypt with the Lord's promise of making his family a great nation with a great name and abundant blessings with which to bless others. But then things traveled south, literally. We discover the first of three situations where men pass their wives off as their sisters—twice with Abram and Sarai (see Genesis 12:10–20; 20:1–18) and once with Isaac and Rebekah (Genesis 26:1–16). What was the motivation for this rather odd act? Perhaps both men focused on themselves and became afraid for their own lives, while at the same time putting their wives in danger. Each wife-as-sister ruse occurred directly after God promised these patriarchs and their families lives of commitment, blessings, and prosperity.

Abram himself offered an interesting excuse. He claimed that he was in fact Sarai's brother, that they had the same father but not the same mother (Genesis 20:12). Yet a half-truth is a whole lie. Abram's intent was clearly deceptive, in which he trusted his deception, not the Lord, would protect him.

Sarai was taken to Pharaoh to be his wife and part of his harem. In return, Abram was blessed with sheep, oxen, donkeys, camels, and servants! As a result, God plagued Pharaoh's house. Before Pharaoh sent Abram and Sarai from Egypt, he offered them protection on their way out. Surprisingly, Pharaoh's concern for Sarai seemed more sincere than Abram's.

In all they experienced while in Egypt, imagine the trauma Sarai faced and tension it must have put on Abram and Sarai's relationship. In today's culture, imagine the negative effects of deception within families who encounter similar situations as Abram and Sarai faced. Consider the difficulties facing state and local children's services and social workers in placing and caring for children from planned or unplanned blended families. Even in the midst of Abram's disobedience, the Lord kept his promises to Abram and Sarai and their generations, and the Lord will keep his promise of protecting your family members too.

In Genesis 16:1–15, ten years had passed since God's promise that a family—a great nation—would come from Abram and Sarai, and nothing had happened yet; they gave up on the Lord's plan. Follow the bouncing ball of results when Abram and Sarai decided to take things into their own hands:

- Barren Sarai suggested Abram have a child with her servant, Hagar (who was one of the Egyptians given to Abram in exchange for Sarai).
- Hagar became pregnant and assumed she now had God's favor instead of Sarai, so the servant looked down on Sarai with disrespect and contempt.
- Jealousy enraged Sarai, which caused her to blame Abram.
- In response, Abram did not want any responsibility from his actions, so he passed the blame back to Sarai, telling her to do whatever she wants with Hagar.
- Sarai mistreated Hagar (no in-depth details are given), causing Hagar to run away.

Wow, does this remind you of another Genesis family—Adam and Eve? These are some of the same emotions and outward responses that have passed down the generational line. Even though Sarai's and Hagar's culture was different than ours, they were women with the same feelings women have today. Wives, how would you react and how would you feel—emotionally, physically, mentally, and spiritually—if another woman became pregnant by your husband? Men, do you believe those feelings and possible reactions to be consistent of the women close to you?

There is no *fun* in this dys*fun*ctional situation and family that Abram, Sarai, and Hagar faced. God's plans are always for our best, even if our plans are much different. If God gives a promise, he will keep it. Like Abram and Sarai, we may choose not to wait for God's plan or may think God forgot because things aren't happening when we expect them to. We may doubt God, even though there is no doubt he will keep his promises. And because the Lord always keeps his promises, he intervened in Hagar's life and told her to return to Abram's house. She named her son Ishmael, which means, *God hears*. In turn she gave the Lord a name: you are a *God who sees* me (in Hebrew, *El-Ro'i*). *The God who sees* her in turmoil and with a messed-up life will also take care of her and her child.

Thankfully, God always keeps his word. His promises cannot be thwarted by your present situation, your past, your emotional, physical, mental scars, and cannot even be thwarted by the actions of your family toward you. God sees you. God hears you. God loves you. God acts favorably on your behalf because of his love for you.

In Genesis 17:1–21 and 18:9–15, with the covenant marked by circumcision comes a new name for Abram: Abraham, which means *father of many nations*. God changed Sarai's name to Sarah, meaning *princess*. Abraham is ninety-nine and Sarah is eighty-nine. When God told them that Sarah would have a child in her old age, Abraham laughed. Sarah laughed too. But

God had the last laugh when he asked, "Is anything too hard for the Lord?" (Genesis 18:14).

In Genesis 21:1–14, God kept his promise to give Abraham and Sarah a child. No surprise there! Abraham (age one hundred) and Sarah (age ninety) are blessed with a child, Isaac, which means *he laughs.* Sarah predicted people would laugh at her, having a child at her age. And sure enough, someone did— Ishmael (Abraham and Hagar's son). Sarah had had enough. She instructed Abraham to send Hagar and Ishmael away, not wanting Ishmael to share in his rightful inheritance as firstborn. Reluctantly, Abraham sent Hagar and Ishmael (now fourteen years old) on their way to wander in the wilderness, carrying with them the Lord's promise that he would make Ishmael a nation because he was also Abraham's offspring.

Ishmael might fit into the statistics of the modern world. It would be interesting to see his score on the ACEs survey. Consider the statistics of today's children in Ishmael-like situations. Various groups and studies report that a large majority (70–90 percent) of

- children who exhibit behavioral disorders come from fatherless homes.
- homeless and runaway children are from fatherless homes.
- adolescent patients in chemical abuse centers come from fatherless homes.

- juveniles in state-operated institutions come from fatherless homes.

According to research from the ACEs documentary, *Paper Tigers*, about childhood trauma, all the risk factors for adverse experiences can be offset by one thing: the presence of a stable, caring adult in a child's life. Children need the love and influence of both mother and father. The lack of one of those parents will have a significant impact on the development of a child. Discuss this insight as you consider Ishmael's life, the children in your community, and your own life.

Consider. Discuss. Apply It to Your Life and Community.

Why is God's response important for you to hear at this time in your life or the lives of your family? Do you believe and trust that nothing is too difficult for the Lord? Have you laughed at God's ways and promises for your life?

_____

_____

_____

_____

Abraham waited a long time to see God's promise of making his family a great nation. How long would you wait for the Lord to bring his promises to fruition in your life? How difficult do you find it to trust God's promises within your family?

_____

_____

_____

_____

What are some of God's promises you may have forgotten, doubted, or disbelieved?

_____

_____

_____

_____

How does the knowledge that God always keeps his word change your outlook as you move forward? Consider memorizing Genesis 16:13.

_____

_____

_____

_____

Would you be willing to *champion* or mentor a child in jeopardy? Who has served as your champion or mentor throughout your life, either intentionally or by their caring example?

_____

_____

_____

_____

Remember that our God who sees and hears promises us, as God's people, that he will never leave us or forsake us (Deuteronomy 31:6–8), and nothing can separate us from the love of God in Jesus Christ our Lord (Romans 8:37–39). How do these promises from your perfect Father encourage you as you walk with God?

_____

_____

_____

_____

Pray. Encourage. Move Forward, Filled with Hope.

In preparation for the next lesson, read Genesis 13:1–13; 14:10–16; 19:1–38.

Lesson 5

LOT'S FAMILY: A LOT OF SIN AND A LOT OF HELP

Read Genesis 13:1–13; 14:10–16; 19:1–38.

IMAGINE IF YOU HAD a lot of money, land, and *stuff*. Now imagine a lot of people taking care of *your* stuff. That was the reality of life for Lot and his uncle Abraham in Genesis 13:1–13. And it led to a lot of family (and employee) arguments. Therefore, Abraham and Lot decided it would be best to separate. Lot took his family, along with the workers and livestock, and traveled east to the Jordan Valley and the region of Sodom. Abraham's family and several hundred servants stayed in Canaan. Perhaps you can relate to their stress. Let's make this personal for a minute.

It doesn't matter if they are small or large, tension and arguments plague most families. In family tension or arguments, each family member takes on the role of hero, rescuer, mediator/peacemaker, scapegoat, power broker, nurturer, or guilt provider. Conversely, some family members band together to resolve the conflict.

Genesis 18 provides a backstory to Sodom, where Lot and his family lived. Then in Genesis 14:10–16 and Genesis 19:1–29, we find that after some time, outsiders overtook the area. Abraham received word that kings and armies had taken Lot and his possessions. Lot was family. Abraham and his trained men rescued and returned Lot to his home.

Lot welcomed two men (angels sent by the Lord) to Sodom and into his home, not realizing they were sent by God. All the men of Sodom surrounded the house, wanting the two men for sexual purposes. Shockingly, Lot offered the crowd of men his virgin daughters instead. But they were only interested in the men. They stormed the house, and the angels confused the crowd with blindness. Having been sent by the Lord to destroy the city because its people sinned so grievously, the two messengers insisted Lot and his family leave immediately (Genesis 18:20).

While the lives of the people in Genesis are often so troubling and it's difficult to relate to our family's lives today, Lot's story is especially heinous. Although appalling, offering one's children for selfish gain or safety isn't unheard of. Today's parents have been known to sell their children for drugs, money, and sex, including sex trafficking.

Even though God saved Lot's family, Lot decided, out of selfishness and fear, to trust his own plan over God's (Genesis 19:19). The Lord told him to go one way, but Lot chose another. He and his daughters eventually lived in a cave, shut off from the world, and definitely not where God wanted them to safely be. Lot's wife, like so many of us, ignored God's commands. We either don't trust God, or we can't walk away from our past. We become so deeply rooted and trapped in our sin that we don't want to let go. We cling to the good memories we had while we were in it. We like "fitting in" with those around us who have chosen to ignore God. Like Lot's wife, we look back, even though God commands us not to. Instead of moving forward in freedom with God, we look back and find ourselves dead in our tracks.

In Genesis 19:30–38 we find, once again, drunkenness and sex (incest in this case) playing a major role in the life of a parent, children, and grandchildren. Because there were no men in the mountains where Lot and his daughters lived, they wanted to ensure Lot's future offspring. They enticed Lot into a drunken stupor and slept with him, therefore becoming pregnant by their father. Consider the repercussions throughout the lives of Lot, his daughters, and his grandchildren, who were also his children.

Sexual and emotional abuse are two of the ten types of adversities examined in the ACEs study. Children who suffer childhood trauma specific to the ten considered from the ACEs study will often suffer long-term trauma. This affects how they will respond to future stressful situations. Even though Lot's daughters weren't raped, they were still traumatized by being offered as a sacrifice. Those who have never been sexually abused may think this would cause sexual aversion in a victim. However, most often the case is the opposite. Risky sexual behavior is common among those who have been sexually victimized.

To avoid this risky behavior from sexual and emotional abuse, we find help in 1 Corinthians 10:13, where Jesus promises, "No temptation has overtaken you that is not common to man. God is faithful, and he will not let you be tempted beyond your ability, but with the temptation he will also provide the way of escape, that you may be able to endure it."

The story of Lot and Abraham and Lot and his daughters are challenging portions of Scripture. We see God's love that wanted to protect Lot and his family from those dangers. God offered Lot and his family a way to freedom. While Lot, his wife, and his daughters did not always follow that freedom road, God remained faithful. His eternal love was undeserving, unfathomable, and often unappreciated.

God doesn't shy away from sharing the realities of human weakness and our affinities toward temptation in the Bible. We are all sinners and have broken every command of God. There is no difference. All sin is equal. If we've broken one of God's laws, we've broken them all. But Christ took all our sins and the punishment due us on himself when he went to the cross. Christ took Lot's sin and the sins of his family; he took my sin, your sin, and the sins of the world. And in return, he gives us forgiveness as a most grace-filled gift to all who receive it in faith.

Consider. Discuss. Apply It to Your Life and Community.

As you grew up, how did you observe your family deal with conflict? Did you have a role, and has that role changed over the years? Or did your family band together?

_____

_____

_____

_____

What have you observed about tensions, temptation, and arguments in various socioeconomic groups?

_____

_____

_____

_____

Genesis 14:14 tells us the size of Abraham and Sarah's household was a large community almost like an army. How much of a role did your "community" (e.g., church, relatives, friends, classmates) play in your childhood? How important is community for healthy and/or dysfunctional families?

_____

_____

_____

_____

What is your family's view of and/or involvement with other trained servants in your larger community, such as police, social workers, family services, clergy, professional counselors, rehab centers, and others?

_____

_____

_____

_____

What long-term emotional effects could children sold for another's selfish reasons struggle with?

_____

_____

_____

_____

We have been warned of grave consequences and destruction, yet we often see grace and rescue, the message of Genesis 19:16, played out in our lives. What is your personal *Sodom* or that of your family? What sin has taken over your life?

_____

_____

_____

_____

When do you find it easy to follow God's will? When you do find it difficult to move forward and follow Jesus?

_____

_____

_____

_____

Keeping in mind the story of God protecting Lot despite his faithlessness, when has God's grace (undeserved love) overwhelmed you, grown your faith, and given you a hope-filled future overflowing with praise and thanks?

_____

_____

_____

_____

Pray. Encourage. Move Forward, Filled with Hope.

In preparation for the next lesson, read Genesis 25:19–34; 29:1–35; 30:1–24.

Lesson 6

Jacob's Relationships: More Tricks Than Treats

Read Genesis 25:19–34; 29:1–35; 30:1–24.

WE FIND IN GENESIS 25:28 that Isaac and Rebekah favored one child over another. The passage is not suggesting they loved one and not the other, but rather, between the parents existed a divided loyalty for each child. Each parent favored a different child.

However, in Genesis 29:1–30, as we follow Jacob's life, we discover his shortcomings included lying, deceit, and manipulation. Yet God had chosen Jacob to play an important role in his plan for his people and even salvation through his descendant, Jesus. Throughout Old Testament history, the people of God held their forefathers in esteem as God's chosen leaders. References to "the God of Abraham, Isaac, and Jacob" are numerous.

During Bible times, the birthright of the firstborn included many privileges and played an important role in the life of the family. The firstborn's birthright included a double portion of the inheritance, leadership over the family, and a blessing to carry on the covenant promises.

Apparently, deceit ran in Jacob's family's DNA, as he met his match in his uncle Laban, who toyed with the lives, relationships, and emotions of his daughters and nephew (Genesis 29:23–25). Jacob wasn't sheepish about proclaiming his love for Laban's daughter, Rachel, a shepherdess. Jacob agreed to work for Laban for seven years to marry Rachel. At least that's what he thought. Perhaps veils, cloth, dim lighting, and blind love played a part in the ole switcheroo trick. It wasn't until the next day that Laban told Jacob that his people always marry the oldest daughter first. Unaware, Jacob had married Leah instead of Rachel. It was another seven years of work until Jacob finally married his dear Rachel. The deceiver met his deceiving match in another reoccurring, sinful cycle that had passed down through the family line.

Genesis 29:31–30:24 shows us the results of playing selfish games. Games should be reserved for baby showers, and should not be played with the lives of innocent babies to soothe an adult's personal pride or selfishness. This section of Scripture boils down to a baby game. A competition based on jealousy was played out, at least for an insecure Leah. Perhaps she hoped to earn the love of a man and heal her marriage. Full of jealousy, barren Rachael was the first to offer her servant to Jacob in hopes of having children in her own family. These children, born to satisfy the insecure longings of a barren womb or jealousy of another's fruitful womb, would later be the heads of the twelve tribes of Israel. Twelve children from one man and four women: Leah, Rachel, and their servants, who played the role of surrogate mothers.

It's not uncommon for a teen pregnancy to become like a baby game, a competition between friends or relatives, especially those longing for love or looking for acceptance. When one teen couple gives birth, another teen may desire the same for themselves and want that experience as well, so they follow suit. Some teens desire a child, with the hope that having the child will make everything all right between their family dysfunction or in their personal world. What they don't realize are the challenges, stress, and sometimes harmful cycles caused by those unhealthy choices and consequences.

Deceit is an-all-too popular theme in the families found in Genesis and in our society. Thankfully, deceit meets defeat by the truth on our lips and in our hearts. God's forgiveness gives birth to the freedom found in Christ. John 8:31–32 speaks of this freedom, "So Jesus said to the Jews who had believed him, 'If you abide in my word, you are truly my disciples, and you will know the truth, and the truth will set you free.'"

Consider. Discuss. Apply It to Your Life and Community.

Discuss the family dynamics, deception, and repercussions in Genesis 25:29–34, including Esau's lie and Jacob's manipulative ways.

_____

_____

_____

_____

What drives the often common but misguided decision of using babies or children with the intent to restore a relationship? How might this decision influence the child's life?

_____

_____

_____

_____

Jacob's sons, born to servants Zilpah and Bilhah, can be likened to children born today by surrogates or in vitro fertilization (IVF) and raised by kinship providers, or those who are adopted, or are half-siblings. What are possible blessings and challenges for such children and their families?

_____

_____

_____

_____

Discuss the obvious challenges of child-parents, who are often completely unprepared to raise children. How can parents, educators, churches, organizations, and individuals prepare, inform, and help children having children?

_____

_____

_____

_____

One of the greatest challenges facing the child welfare system today, as well as extended biological families, is individuals having children with multiple partners. Discuss the dynamics, similarities, and differences regarding Jacob's family and modern ones. Include your childhood and adult family experiences. Topics to consider might include supporting, providing, and protecting children; absentee parenting; long-term plans and goals for a family; and why this issue has changed public health and child welfare.

_____

_____

_____

_____

Pray. Encourage. Move Forward, Filled with Hope.

In preparation for the next lesson, read Genesis 35:1–7; 37:1–36; 38:1–30; 45:1–11; 50:15–21. (Recommended reading: Genesis 37:1–50:26.)

Lesson 7

JACOB'S FAMILY TREE
BEARS CURSES AND
BLESSINGS

Read Genesis 35:1–29; 37:1–36; 38:1–30; 45:1–11; 50:15–21. (Recommended reading: 37:1–50:26, and see chapters 34, 42–45.)

GOD GAVE JACOB A new name, Israel, after his experience of wrestling with God (Genesis 32:22–32). It is restated in 35:10. In the paragraphs that follow, both names are used.

The story of Jacob's family, especially as it addresses his son Joseph, the firstborn son of his true love, Rachel, is one of the most extensive in all of Scripture. While you read the beginning accounts of his family, consider reading the rest of Genesis (chapters 37–50) on your own or as a group. The last two chapters of Genesis (49 and 50) include the blessings Jacob bestowed on each of his sons just before his death, as well as his sons' individual responses to his death. In all these chapters you will see the grace Joseph shows his brothers—pointing them to their sovereign God. In many ways, the final chapters reveal how Joseph's faith, evident throughout his life, broke the cycle of great family dysfunction that had passed down through generations.

These foundational verses in Genesis 35:1–15 remind us of God's great love for Jacob in calling the patriarch to turn his family and faith toward the Lord. They also describe Jacob's relationship with the Lord and their desire that his household, including his children, servants, and traveling companions recommit their lives to the Lord.

In Genesis 35:16–29, Rachel dies while giving birth to the last of Jacob's children. As she is dying, Rachel names him Ben-oni (meaning *son of my sorrow*). After her death, Jacob renames him Benjamin (meaning *son of my right hand*), likely so the name Ben-oni wouldn't be a constant reminder of the death of the love of his life, Rachel. Not long after Rachel's death, Jacob's father, Isaac, dies. Jacob and Esau bury their father (Genesis 35:27–29).

The list of Jacob's blended family, below, is complicated—twelve boys and one girl. Jacob is the father of all thirteen, born to four different women (35:22–26). The birth order of each child is noted in parenthesis:

> Leah, Jacob's wife: Reuben (1), Simeon (2), Levi (3), Judah (4), Issachar (9), Zebulun (10), Dinah (11)

Zilpah (Leah's servant): Gad (7), Asher (8)

Bilhah (Rachel's servant): Dan (5), Naphtali (6)

Rachel, Jacob's wife: Joseph (12), Benjamin (13)

Inserted in Genesis 35:22, in an almost casual way, is the story of Reuben having an affair with Bilhah, who was a servant of his stepmother, Rachel. Though briefly mentioned, it is not intended as an insignificant sinful action in the story, because it impacted the family and their relationships. Furthermore, Reuben's sexual sin caused him to lose his birthright as the first-born son (Genesis 49:3–4).

The biblical account in Genesis 37:1–36 of Joseph's relationship with his brothers begins when he was a teenager at seventeen. Throughout the years prior, the jealousy and hatred between them had grown and worsened because their family dynamics were complicated and deep-rooted, as outlined below:

- Rape: Dinah, the only daughter, was humiliated and raped (34:1–31).
- Murder, protecting their sister: Simeon and Levi, Dinah's brothers, tricked the rapist, killed him, looted his home, and took family members hostage.
- Death of a parent: Rachel died giving birth to Jacob's youngest son, Benjamin (35:16–21).

- Sexual sin: After Rachel's death, her step-son Rueben had sexual relations with her servant, Bilhah (35:22).
- Family hostility, sibling rivalry, anger: When Joseph was seventeen years old, he told his dad, Jacob, some of the bad things his brothers were doing. The resulting resentment and jealously within their family wasn't something new, considering how those traits were shared between their four birth mothers, along with their father (37:2).
- Jealousy: Jacob loved Joseph more than his other children, and they all knew it. He even made Joseph an elaborate, colorful robe (37:3–4).
- Humiliation, insults, jealousy, and hatred: Joseph's brothers were jealous of and hated him. They couldn't have a civil conversation with him. Their hatred for Joseph grew more and more intense, especially after he told them about the dreams in which they bowed down to him (37:5–11).
- Hatred, abuse, abandonment, lies, and betrayal: The hatred Joseph's brothers showed grew so great they devised a plan to kill him by throwing him into a pit and telling his father and others that an animal had

attacked him. The oldest, Rueben, stopped their plan (37:18–36).

This is quite a list. Makes me wonder what our family list would look like if we were to reveal what each of our family members are guilty of? Think about your parents, spouse, siblings, children, and yourself. Yet faithfulness offers redemption from even the worst of our sins.

If you read or know the stories in Genesis 45:1–11 and 50:15–21 of Joseph being sold into slavery, you know the good news. God used Egypt's leader (Pharaoh) and the gifts of faith, wisdom, and grace to raise up Joseph to be the second-most powerful man in the country. A famine brought Jacob's family from Canaan to Egypt, where they found help and grace from their brother and son, Joseph, even though they didn't recognize him at the time. Through the most unlikely of events, God brought Jacob's family reconciliation, forgiveness, and healing as described in Colossians 1:13–14: "He has delivered us from the domain of darkness and transferred us to the kingdom of his beloved Son, in whom we have redemption, the forgiveness of sins."

This is a large and complicated family. Many of ours are as well. Jacob's family could have been the entire Bible study, but we chose to show that brokenness in families reaches most households in some way. Therefore we used multiple biblical stories. We are going to offer many more questions for discussion than is common to most studies. Your group may want to spend more time or divide the questions into smaller groups.

Consider. Discuss. Apply It to Your Life and Community.

How has grief played a role in your family dynamics as a child and as an adult? How have your family members dealt with their grief?

_____

_____

_____

_____

What dynamics come into play with blended families? What are the blessings, and what makes blending complicated?

_____

_____

_____

_____

How have sinful actions impacted the relationships and dynamics within your family?

_____

_____

_____

_____

God commissioned Jacob to serve as the spiritual leader in his home. What did that involve? What do we learn about the faith of his family and household in Genesis 35:1–7?

_____

_____

_____

_____

What are the promises of God to Jacob/Israel and his descendants in Genesis 35:9–12? How did Jacob respond to the promises and presence of God in Genesis 35:14–15?

_____

_____

_____

_____

How do God's presence, call, and promises in Genesis 35:1–15 echo down the halls of history into our lives and the lives of our families?

_____

_____

_____

_____

Joseph could have easily walked away from God's will, having been tempted by power, money, good looks, and opportunities. Why didn't he succumb to the temptation?

_____

_____

_____

_____

With the ACEs survey in mind, consider the family incidents recorded in Genesis chapters 34–35 and 37. How might similar situations need to be addressed in your family's story?

_____

_____

_____

_____

What speaks most clearly to your heart as you read Genesis 45:1–11 and 50:15–21? How can you apply it to your relationships within (and outside of) your family?

_____

_____

_____

_____

How would you expect adverse experiences and resulting emotions to affect the individuals and relationships within the family, including continuing the cycle of dysfunction?

_____

_____

_____

_____

How can Jesus bring healing, hope, and victory even to the most hurtful and destructive experiences?

_____

_____

_____

_____

How were many of the dysfunctional, sinful family cycles broken because of Joseph's right response toward his family?

_____

_____

_____

_____

What is your hope in seeing how God worked in the story of Joseph, his siblings, and his parents? Who is the source of that hope and good news? Do you see God's story being revealed within your story? Within your family of origin and/or present family?

_____

_____

_____

_____

These words of Joseph are some of the most healing and insightful truths in Scripture: "As for you, you meant evil against me, but God meant it for good, to bring it about that many people should be kept alive, as they are today" (Genesis 50:20). What healing role might these words about God's plan, grace, and forgiveness play in your life during times of pain, hurt, and despair?

_____

_____

_____

_____

What have the family stories in Genesis taught you about individual and family relationships? What have they taught you about God's love, power, presence, and promises?

_____

_____

_____

_____

Pray. Encourage. Move Forward, Filled with Hope.

In preparation for the next lesson, read Romans 8:1–39; 12:1–21.

Lesson 8

ROOTED IN THE MOST GNARLED, UNHEALTHY, LEFT-FOR-DEAD FAMILY TREE

Read Romans 8:1–39; 12:1–21.

GENEALOGIES—FAMILY TREES—ARE PLANTED NOT only in the book of Genesis but throughout the entire Old Testament. Most people perceive family genealogy lists to be unimportant and irrelevant to today's life and faith, yet these lists are significant and tell the story of God's undeserved love, which impacts our lives and our faith in great ways! The listing of names and families can even encourage us in our faith. God created, cared about, blessed, and gave hope to families by sending his Son to lay down his life for them on a "family" tree outside of Jerusalem so he could spend eternity with them in paradise.

Family trees in Scripture (see also Matthew 1 and Luke 3) point to Jesus. They are rooted in the soil of God's truth, promises, and faithfulness, and would bear the fruit of the One promised to Adam, Eve,

Abraham, Judah, David, and their families. God gave his word, and he does not lie (Titus 1:2). His steadfast love and faithfulness are themes throughout Scripture.

Genealogies remind us that God cares about history and *his* story within the world. They show us God interacts with and is present in the lives of real people—real, sinful people. And he loves them with a real love. They remind us that God cares about, understands, and values families, yours included. Even if you described your family as dysfunctional, God is not; neither is he uncaring, unaware, or unavailable. He is completely caring, aware, and available to you and your family.

Take note of some of the individuals and families connected by grace in the Messiah's gnarled, unhealthy, left-for-dead family tree, as recorded in Matthew 1:1–17 and Luke 3:23–38. These people are more than names. Each name presents a story. Some stories are twisted and unhealthy, while some overflow, filled with acts of faithfulness and obedience. God is working in every life. His story is a part of their story.

In the Old Testament, you have seen the lives of Adam and Eve, Noah, Abraham, Isaac, Jacob, and their family members. You also found several wicked kings and some who went from faithful to unfaithful. You discovered both Jews and Gentiles in the family tree of the King of the Jews. And while women were not included in any Old Testament genealogies, God noted them in his Son's family tree, along with the sinful men. Four were Gentiles. Tamar tricked Judah, her father-in-law, into a sexual relationship. Rahab was a prostitute who helped God's servants escape death. Ruth was a Moabite. David and Bathsheba, the wife of Uriah and mother of Solomon, had an affair. And there is, of course, Mary, the girl who gave birth to the promised Messiah.

You've taken a small glimpse into the family rooms of our Savior's Genesis ancestors through this study. Hopefully, through the dysfunction and pain, you saw the steadfast love and faithfulness of God. You also read about God's people's great acts of faith, not just their sinfulness. God's faithfulness to his people and his promises remained constant, through even their most grievous sins. And God's faithfulness is the same today in the stories of our family trees and for the person we see in the mirror, a just and faithful God with a steadfast love, forgiving our grievous and vile sins. Consider the following passages that put all our sins into God's perspective:

> For whoever keeps the whole law but fails in one point has become guilty of all of it.
> (James 2:10)

> There is no difference between Jew and Gentile, for all have sinned and fall short of the glory of God, and all are justified freely by his grace through the redemption that came by

Christ Jesus. God presented Christ as a sacrifice of atonement, through the shedding of his blood—to be received by faith.
(Romans 3:22–25 NIV)

God's grace bestowed on the patriarchs and their families in Genesis is also gratefully realized in our lives. John writes, "If we say we have no sin, we deceive ourselves, and the truth is not in us. If we confess our sins, he is faithful and just to forgive us our sins and to cleanse us from all unrighteousness. If we say we have not sinned, we make him a liar, and his word is not in us" (1 John 1:8–10).

As we consider the parents in Genesis, may we be reminded of the words in Proverbs 22:6: "Train up a child in the way he should go; even when he is old he will not depart from it."

Training and raising children is the most important, intentional commitment of the Christ-centered parent. Parents are to teach their children God's Word, his ways, and his will. The proverb implies that the outcome will be that even when the child is old, he or she will not depart from it—that this training will have a permanent effect on a child. This is not a magical formula or a hard-and-fast promise.

While this verse is framed as an instruction to parents, the book of Proverbs gives guidance to youth also (Proverbs 4:1). Proverbs teaches that a child's future depends not only on the parents' guidance, but also on the choices the child makes. According to Proverbs 2:12–19, anyone may refuse God's grace and turn from God's way. Noah, Abraham, and all parents are called to train the children entrusted to them in God's Word and ways, to lead by example, to pray for them, forgive them and ask for their forgiveness, and to love them as Christ loves us. At times we will fail as parents and as children, so we can only pray for wisdom while relying on and giving thanks for God's good news and grace.

Starting with Adam and Eve's rebellion, God's plan for his people included his living Son dying on a cross-shaped tree for the sins of the world and for everyone in his family tree. Jesus was the perfect sacrifice for our sins and that of our families'. But God's plan didn't end at the cross. Three days after his sacrificial death, he rose from the dead, securing a resurrection and eternal life for his children. And his ascension into heaven ultimately points to the return of Jesus in glory when God's good work begun in us will be completed (Philippians 1:6). As a result, all creation will be set free from decay and death and given over to a perfect life with the perfect family, the redeemed and reconciled family of God found in Romans 8. Those who place their Spirit-created faith in God's Son will stand before God the Father covered with the perfection of Jesus.

There is hope.

There is good news.

There is forgiveness.

There is reconciliation.

There is an abundant life.

There is an eternal life.

All because of and only through Jesus.

That's news the Holy Spirit shares with you and your family—not just for you to know, but for you to hold on to for life.

Pray. Encourage. Move Forward, Filled with Hope.

WRAP UP: NOW WHAT?

Norman Rockwell painted many pictures depicting perfect-looking families. One famous piece of art shows a loving family sitting down for a meal. You won't find any perfect families you met in this study of Genesis sitting down for a meal of goat, fruit, and honey. Obviously, that's because the perfect Genesis family doesn't exist! The families found in the book of Genesis were far from perfect, as are our families. The families in the book of Genesis had secrets in their animal skin-covered closets and cycles of sin in their histories. They were broken families *just like ours,* in need of redemption, reconciliation, and forgiveness from a just, faithful, and compassionate God with a perfect plan of salvation through one to be born of a woman, as God promised Eve in Genesis 3:15. Living beyond the manger, cross, and resurrection, we know that the promised One is God's own Son and the world's Savior, Jesus Christ, who overcame our imperfections.

Jesus understands when your patience wears thin (maybe your child won't stop crying). His patience was pushed to the brink also when he entered the temple and found it seemingly turned into a market (John 2:13–16). He was exhausted, but he took the time to help a Samaritan woman when she came to draw water from the physical well, and he gave her living water (John 4:6). Visualize him with his disciples as they argued over who was the greatest. You'll realize Jesus knows, as you do, how difficult relationships can be (Luke 22:24–26). He knows. He understands. He has the power to reconcile and restore past relationships.

Forgiveness through Jesus frees his people to live abundantly. He will not let you be tempted in a way you cannot handle. And he will always provide a way to escape from temptations, as 1 Corinthians 10:13 promises.

As you consider your Adverse Childhood Experiences, have you allowed the Holy Spirit to open the door of forgiveness in your life? Forgiveness isn't always easy for us, but it's easy for our Savior. He leaves us an example in his free and full forgiveness of our sins. Some people may find it difficult to forgive because they think that if they forgive someone, they are saying that what the person did was right or okay. That's not what forgiveness means. Sin is never right or okay. Sin is never God's will. As we realize how much God has forgiven us in Jesus, we want to respond by forgiving those who may have hurt us so that we will be free to live as Christ intends. Through that forgiveness, we can pray that same forgiveness for others. Through God's forgiveness, we realize the peace of God in our lives—a peace only he can give—and that allows us to be able to move beyond the sin. Harboring anger and bitterness are not attributes that God has planned for your abundant life in Jesus. Here's the question again: As you consider your Adverse Childhood Experiences, have you allowed the Holy Spirit to open the door of forgiveness in your life?

In addition, Jesus also provides help for life in a sinful world through organizations that support parents and champion children through advocates and through educational opportunities and tools that build skills for coping in life.

Maybe you have a need to ask your pastor or Christ-centered friends for suggestions of counselors to help in your healing so you may enjoy the abundant life Jesus has in store for you.

As an adult, recognizing how many ACEs you encountered as a child is necessary to understanding our own minds, hearts, and health. Recognizing a problem leads to discovering a solution, and acknowledging and addressing our ACEs score teaches and helps us move forward in healthy, Christ-centered relationships and families. The health of our families is the health of our nation.

Next Steps

Discuss your hope and/or plan as a group, a church, a mission community, or as individuals to strengthen and heal your family and relationships and help others (of every age) who are struggling and in need of guidance. Seek support organizations specializing in family issues. Keep the eyes of your faith open to see how God is leading you to have a heart for those around you in need of hope and help.

Although not exhaustive, consider the following list of action points and resource links to help and encourage you as a member of the faith-based community.

Education

Consider creating parenting and child development education at your church if it is not available in your community or high schools. This opportunity can be offered for those already in the trenches who need help or for youth who may be parents in the future. Encourage and advocate in your community or schools to prioritize this type of education. The public outcry for change is where movements begin. Also, consult with your church's youth/student ministries about providing education in coping skills, family dynamics, faith within families, teen pregnancy, and parenting skills. You may need to begin by contacting your local high school to check if they offer any parenting or child development education.

Adoption

Adoption is a celebrated way of creating or enlarging a family. How might your group or church support and encourage adoption options and families considering adoption? Consider ways to support children awaiting adoption. Adoption can be key to a child's identity, hope, faith, and life. The church could offer adoption/foster agencies the opportunity to speak to its membership or individual groups.

Resource: http://www.americanadoptions.com/adoption/adoption-definition

Foster Care

The foster care system is a temporary arrangement in which adults provide for the care of a child or children whose birth parent is unable to care for them. Some may view foster care as where juvenile delinquents are placed, but this is not accurate.

Foster care can be informal or arranged through the courts or by a social service agency. The goal for a child placed in the foster care system is usually reunification with the birth family. But adoption of foster children is an option when it is in the child's best interest. While foster care is temporary, adoption is permanent.

Adoption/foster agencies are often in need of personal items for these children in their care. Many families who open their doors to children appreciate help with clothing, personal items, toys, diapers, wipes, and school supplies, to name a few items. Would your church or group consider partnering with a local agency or starting your own supply support for foster families?

Resource: http://www.adopt.org/what-foster-care

Kinship Provider

A kinship provider is an option extended from the foster care program in which a relative or one who has a close relationship with the family cares for a child(ren) whose birthparent(s) is unable to do so themselves. Kinship fostering is a preference for all agencies involved. The trauma of a child being removed from the only home, family, and environment they know can be reduced if the child is placed with someone who is familiar to them. Examples of kinship are grandparents, aunts and uncles, older siblings, teachers, coaches, or church families.

Note: Foster (including kinship foster) and adoptive parents may be single, married, divorced, widowed, or partners who are age twenty-one and over and are able to provide for a household. They are made up of all ages, races, and religions.

Resource: https://www.fosteradopt.org/independence-mo/programs/licensing/

Respite Care Provider

Respite care provides parents and other caregivers with short-term childcare services that offer temporary relief, improve family stability, and reduce the risk of abuse or neglect. Respite can be planned or offered during emergencies or times of crisis. Respite may be available to foster, kinship, and adoptive families, as well as birth families in need of support. You may need to make your church community aware of this program in which they could serve as a provider.

Resource: https://www.childwelfare.gov/topics/preventing/prevention-programs/respite/

Advocate

CASA (Court Appointed Special Advocates) is one advocacy group in need of volunteers. A special degree or background is not required. Volunteers are thoroughly trained and well supported by professional staff.

Volunteers working with children are active in all aspects of the child's life (e.g., family members, foster parents, teachers, medical professionals, attorneys, social workers). They gather information that helps judges and others decide on the best options for the child's permanent family placement. Children, who previously had no voice in the courtroom, can be heard through their CASA advocates. Volunteering as little as five hours a week to a CASA child can make a great difference in his or her life. Nearly 700,000 children experience abuse or neglect each year. With a Court Appointed Special Advocate (CASA) or guardian ad litem (GAL) volunteer dedicated to their case,

America's most vulnerable children will have someone speaking up for their best interests.

Resource: http://www.casaforchildren.org/site/c. mtJSJ7MPIsE/b.5301295/k.BE9A/Home.htm

Mentoring

Mentoring programs match an adult role model to a struggling youth. These programs can be set up with intervention or prevention models. Individuals within churches can form mentoring groups. Existing mentoring programs can also provide training. Church groups may partner with an existing agency, school, or organization to provide volunteers. Church leadership can partner with school leadership in guiding youth who are in need to your church group.

Additional Helpful Resources

CDC, https://www.cdc.gov/violenceprevention/ acestudy/index.html

ACE Connection, http://www.ACEsconnection. com/

ACEs Score, https://ACEstoohigh.com/got-your-ace-score/

Paper Tigers, ACE documentary (KPJR Films)

Big Think, https://bigthink.com/experts/vincent-felitti

ACE Interface, http://www.aceinterface.com/ Robert_Anda.html

COPE24, https://cope24.com/

(Offer resources for students, teachers, and parents in speaker series, professional development options, workshops, programs, and faith-based / church-initiative resources.)

Appendix

ENCOURAGEMENT AND GUIDANCE FROM GOD'S WORD

BE BLESSED AND STRENGTHENED by these words from Scripture in your daily walk, following the lead of your Savior, Jesus Christ.

> But when the time arrived that was set by God the Father, God sent his Son, born among us of a woman, born under the conditions of the law so that he might redeem those of us who have been kidnapped by the law. Thus we have been set free to experience our rightful heritage. You can tell for sure that you are now fully adopted as his own children because God sent the Spirit of his Son into our lives crying out, "Papa! Father!" Doesn't that privilege of intimate conversation with God make it plain that you are not a slave, but a child? And if you are a child, you're also an heir, with complete access to the inheritance. (Galatians 4:4–7 MSG)

Is anything too hard for the Lord?
(Genesis 18:14)

Come to me, all who labor and are heavy
laden, and I will give you rest.
(Matthew 11:28)

Trust in the Lord with all your heart, and do
not lean on your own understanding. In all
your ways acknowledge him, and he will make
straight your paths. (Proverbs 3:5–6)

See what kind of love the Father has given to
us, that we should be called children of God;
and so we are. (1 John 3:1)

> The steadfast love of the LORD never ceases;
> > his mercies never come to an end;
> they are new every morning;
> > great is your faithfulness.
> "The Lord is my portion," says my soul,
> > "therefore I will hope in him."
> (Lamentations 3:22–24)

[Jesus said,] Peace I leave with you; my peace
I give to you. Not as the world gives do I give
to you. Let not your hearts be troubled, neither let them be afraid. (John 14:27)

For nothing will be impossible with God.
(Luke 1:37)

Fear not, O Zion;
let not your hands grow weak.
The Lord your God is in your midst,
    a mighty one who will save;
he will rejoice over you with gladness;
    he will quiet you by his love;
he will exult over you with loud singing.
(Zephaniah 3:16–17)

For as many of you as were baptized into Christ have put on Christ. There is neither Jew nor Greek, there is neither slave nor free, there is no male and female, for you are all one in Christ Jesus. And if you are Christ's, then you are Abraham's offspring, heirs according to promise. (Galatians 3:27–29)

Let all bitterness and wrath and anger and clamor and slander be put away from you, along with all malice. Be kind to one another, tenderhearted, forgiving one another, as God in Christ forgave you. (Ephesians 4:31–32)

Come now, let us reason together, says the Lord: though your sins are like scarlet, they shall be as white as snow; though they are red like crimson, they shall become like wool. (Isaiah 1:18)

Therefore, if anyone is in Christ, he is a new creation. The old has passed away; behold, the new has come. (2 Corinthians 5:17)

In him we have redemption through his blood, the forgiveness of our trespasses, according to the riches of his grace, which he lavished upon us, in all wisdom and insight. (Ephesians 1:7–8)

I will remember their sins and their lawless deeds no more. (Hebrews 10:17)

Peace I leave with you; my peace I give to you. Not as the world gives do I give to you. Let not your hearts be troubled, neither let them be afraid. (John 14:27)

I have said these things to you, that in me you may have peace. In the world you will have tribulation. But take heart; I have overcome the world. (John 16:33)

Hear my cry, O God, listen to my prayer;
from the end of the earth I call to you when
my heart is faint.

Lead me to the rock that is higher than I, for you have been my refuge, a strong tower against the enemy. (Psalm 61:1–3)

Have you not known? Have you not heard?
The Lord is the everlasting God,
    the Creator of the ends of the earth.
He does not faint or grow weary;
    his understanding is unsearchable.
He gives power to the faint,
    and to him who has no might he increases strength.
Even youths shall faint and be weary,
    and young men shall fall exhausted;
but they who wait for the Lord shall renew their strength;
    they shall mount up with wings like eagles;
they shall run and not be weary;
    they shall walk and not faint.
(Isaiah 40:28–31)

I do not consider that I have made it my own. But one thing I do: forgetting what lies behind and straining forward to what lies ahead, I press on toward the goal for the prize of the upward call of God in Christ Jesus. (Philippians 3:13–14)

Therefore, since we are surrounded by so great a cloud of witnesses, let us also lay aside every weight, and sin which clings so closely, and let us run with endurance the race that is set before us, looking to Jesus, the founder and perfecter of our faith, who for the joy that was set before him endured the cross, despising the shame, and is seated at the right hand of the throne of God. Consider him who endured from sinners such hostility against himself, so that you may not grow weary or fainthearted. (Hebrews 12:1–3)

For by grace you have been saved through faith. And this is not your own doing; it is the gift of God, not a result of works, so that no one may boast. For we are his workmanship, created in Christ Jesus for good works, which God prepared beforehand, that we should walk in them. (Ephesians 2:8–10)

All this is from God, who through Christ reconciled us to himself and gave us the ministry of reconciliation; that is, in Christ God was reconciling the world to himself, not counting their trespasses against them, and entrusting to us the message of reconciliation. Therefore, we are ambassadors for Christ, God making his appeal through us. We implore you on behalf of Christ, be reconciled to God. For our sake he made him to be sin who knew no sin, so that in him we might become the righteousness of God. (2 Corinthians 5:18–21)

Order Information

REDEMPTION PRESS

To order additional copies of this book, please visit
www.redemption-press.com.
Also available on Amazon.com, BarnesandNoble.com,
and www.cope24.com
Or by calling toll free 1-844-2REDEEM.

CPSIA information can be obtained
at www.ICGtesting.com
Printed in the USA
BVHW070727041118
532065BV00004B/16/P

9 781683 147015